FOR REFERE
(Please do not r

WITH LIBRARY & ARCHIVES

W9-DJJ-936

0 0051 0041349 7

Ella Wheeler Wilcox

OTHER BOOKS

BY

Ella Wheeler Wilcox

EVERY-DAY THOUGHTS

POEMS OF POWER

KINGDOM OF LOVE AND OTHER
    POEMS

THREE WOMEN

MAURINE

POEMS OF PASSION

THE BEAUTIFUL LAND OF NOD

AN ERRING WOMAN'S LOVE

AN AMBITIOUS MAN

MEN, WOMEN AND EMOTIONS

FOR REFERENCE USE ONLY

FOR REFERENCE USE ONLY
(Please do not remove from Library)

POEMS OF PLEASURE

BY

ELLA WHEELER WILCOX

AUTHOR OF

"POEMS OF PASSION," "MAURINE," "EVERY-DAY
THOUGHTS," ETC.

CHICAGO:
W. B. CONKEY COMPANY
1901

UNITY SCHOOL LIBRARY
UNITY VILLAGE, MISSOURI 64065

1888.

COPYRIGHT BY

BELFORD, CLARKE & CO.

1892.

COPYRIGHT BY

MORRILL, HIGGINS & CO.

ALL RIGHTS RESERVED.

1893.

COPYRIGHT BY

W. B. CONKEY COMPANY

ref.
PS
3312
.P5
c.1

CONTENTS.

PASSIONAL.

Poems of Pleasure.

SURRENDER.

LOVE, when we met, 'twas like two planets meet-
   ing.
   Strange chaos followed; body, soul, and heart
Seemed shaken, thrilled, and startled by that greeting.
   Old ties, old dreams, old aims, all torn apart
And wrenched away, left nothing there the while
   But the great shining glory of your smile.

I knew no past; 'twas all a blurred, bleak waste;
   I asked no future; 'twas a blinding glare.
I only saw the present: as men taste
   Some stimulating wine, and lose all care,
I tasted Love's elixir, and I seemed
   Dwelling in some strange land, like one who
      dreamed.

It was a godlike separate existence;
  Our world was set apart in some fair clime.
I had no will, no purpose, no resistance;
  I only knew I loved you for all time.
The earth seemed something foreign and afar,
  And we two, sovereigns dwelling in a star!

It is so sad, so strange, I almost doubt
  That all those years could be, before we met.
Do you not wish that we could blot them out?
  Obliterate them wholly, and forget
That we had any part in life until
  We clasped each other with Love's rapture thrill?

My being trembled to its very center
  At that first kiss.   Cold Reason stood aside
With folded arms to let a grand Love enter
  In my Soul's secret chamber to abide.
Its great High Priest, my first love and my last,
  There on its altar I consumed my past.

And all my life I lay upon its shrine
   The best emotions of my heart and brain,
Whatever gifts and graces may be mine;
   No secret thought, no memory I retain,
But give them all for dear Love's precious sake;
   Complete surrender of the whole I make.

THE BIRTH OF THE OPAL.

THE Sunbeam loved the Moonbeam,
    And followed her low and high,
But the Moonbeam fled and hid her head,
    She was so shy—so shy.

The Sunbeam wooed with passion;
    Ah, he was a lover bold!
And his heart was afire with mad desire
    For the Moonbeam pale and cold.

She fled like a dream before him,
    Her hair was a shining sheen,
And oh, that Fate would annihilate
    The space that lay between!

Just as the day lay panting
    In the arms of the twilight dim,
The Sunbeam caught the one he sought
    And drew her close to him.

But out of his warm arms, startled
   And stirred by Love's first shock,
She sprang afraid, like a trembling maid,
   And hid in the niche of a rock.

And the Sunbeam followed and found her,
   And led her to Love's own feast;
And they were wed on that rocky bed,
   And the dying Day was their priest.

And lo! the beautiful Opal—
   That rare and wondrous gem—
Where the moon and sun blend into one,
   Is the child that was born to them.

THE DIFFERENCE.

PASSION is what the sun feels for the earth
When harvests ripen into golden birth.

Lust is the hot simoon whose burning breath
Sweeps o'er the fields with devastating death.

Passion is what God felt, the Holy One,
Who loved the world so, He begot his Son.

Lust is the impulse Satan peering in
To Eden had, when he taught Eve to sin.

One sprang from light, and one from darkness grew
How dim the vision that confounds the two!

TWO LOVES.

THE woman he loved, while he dreamed of her,
   Danced on till the stars grew dim,
But alone with her heart, from the world apart,
  Sat the woman who loved him.

The woman he worshiped only smiled,
   When he poured out his passionate love.
But the other somewhere, kissed her treasure most
    rare,
   A book he had touched with his glove.

The woman he loved betrayed his trust,
   And he wore the scars for life;
And he cared not, nor knew, that the other was true,
   But no man called her his wife.

The woman he loved trod festal halls,
   While they sang his funeral hymn,
But the sad bells tolled, ere the year was old,
   For the woman who loved him.

THE WAY OF IT.

THIS is the way of it, wide world over,
    One is beloved, and one is the lover,
  One gives and the other receives.
One lavishes all in a wild emotion,
One offers a smile for a life's devotion,
  One hopes and the other believes,
One lies awake in the night to weep,
And the other drifts off in a sweet sound sleep.

One soul is aflame with a godlike passion,
One plays with love in an idler's fashion,
  One speaks and the other hears.
One sobs, "I love you," and wet eyes show it,
And one laughs lightly, and says "I know it."
  With smiles for the other's tears.
One lives for the other and nothing beside,
And the other remembers the world is wide.

This is the way of it, sad earth over,
The heart that breaks is the heart of the lover,
   And the other learns to forget.
"For what is the use of endless sorrow?
Though the sun goes down, it will rise to-morrow;
   And life is not over yet."
Oh! I know this truth, if I know no other,
That passionate Love is Pain's own mother.

ANGEL OR DEMON.

YOU call me an angel of love and of light,
    A being of goodness and heavenly fire,
Sent out from God's kingdom to guide you aright,
    In paths where your spirits may mount and aspire.
You say that I glow like a star on its course,
Like a ray from the altar, a spark from the source.

Now list to my answer; let all the world hear it,
    I speak unafraid what I know to be true:
A pure, faithful love is the creative spirit
    Which makes women angels! I live but in you.
We are bound soul to soul by life's holiest laws;
If I am an angel—why you are the cause.

As my ship skims the sea, I look up from the deck,
    Fair, firm at the wheel shines Love's beautiful form,
And shall I curse the barque that last night went to
        wreck,

By the Pilot abandoned to darkness and storm?
My craft is no stauncher, she too had been lost—
Had the wheelman deserted, or slept at his post.

I laid down the wealth of my soul at your feet
　(Some woman does this for some man every day).
No desperate creature who walks in the street,
　Has a wickeder heart than I might have, I say,
Had you wantonly misused the treasures you won,
—As so many men with heart riches have done.

This fire from God's altar, this holy love flame,
　That burns like sweet incense forever for you,
Might now be a wild conflagration of shame,
　Had you tortured my heart, or been base or untrue.
For angels and devils are cast in one mold,
Till love guides them upward, or downward, I hold.

I tell you the women who make fervent wives
　And sweet tender mothers, had Fate been less fair,
Are the women who might have abandoned their lives

To the madness that springs from and ends in
    despair.
As the fire on the hearth which sheds brightness
    around,
Neglected, may level the walls to the ground.

The world makes grave errors in judging these
    things,
    Great good and great evil are born in one breast.
Love horns us and hoofs us—or gives us our wings,
    And the best could be worst, as the worst could be
    best.
You must thank your own worth for what I grew
    to be,
For the demon lurked under the angel in me.

DAWN.

DAY'S sweetest moments are at dawn;
    Refreshed by his long sleep, the Light
Kisses the languid lips of Night,
Ere she can rise and hasten on.
All glowing from his dreamless rest
He holds her closely to his breast,
Warm lip to lip and limb to limb,
Until she dies for love of him.

PEACE AND LOVE.

THERE are two angels, messengers of light,
    Both born of God, who yet are bitterest foes.
  No human breast their dual presence knows.
As violently opposed as wrong and right,
When one draws near, the other takes swift flight.
    And when one enters, thence the other goes.
    Till mortal life in the immortal flows,
So must these two avoid each other's sight.
Despair and hope may meet within one heart,
The vulture may be comrade to the dove!
Pleasure and Pain swear friendship leal and true:
But till the grave unites them, still apart
Must dwell these angels known as Peace and Love,
For only Death can reconcile the two.

THE INSTRUCTOR.

NOT till we meet with Love in all his beauty,
     In all his solemn majesty and worth,
Can we translate the meaning of life's duty,
     Which God oft writes in cypher at our birth.

Not till Love comes in all his strength and terror,
     Can we read other's hearts; not till then know
A wide compassion for all human error,
     Or sound the quivering depths of mortal woe.

Not till we sail with him o'er stormy oceans,
     Have we seen tempests; hidden in his hand
He holds the keys to all the great emotions;
     Till he unlocks them, none can understand.

Not till we walk with him on lofty mountains,
     Can we quite measure heights. And, oh, sad truth!
When once we drink from his immortal fountains,
     We bid farewell to the light heart of youth.

Thereafter our most perfect day will borrow
   A dimming shadow from some dreaded night.
So great grows joy it merges into sorrow,
   And evermore pain tinctures our delight.

BLASE.

THE world has outlived all its passion,
 Its men are inane and blase,
Its women mere puppets of fashion;
 Life now is a comedy play.
Our Abelard sighs for a season,
 Then yields with decorum to fate.
Our Heloise listens to reason,
 And seeks a new mate.

Our Romeo's flippant emotion
 Grows pale as the summer grows old;
Our Juliet proves her devotion
 By clasping—a cup filled with gold.
Vain Anthony boasts of his favors
 From fair Cleopatra the frail,
And the death of the sorceress savors
 Less of asps than of ale.

With the march of bold civilization,
  Great loves and great faiths are down-trod,
They belonged to an era and nation
  All fresh with the imprint of God.
High culture emasculates feeling,
  The over-taught brain robs the heart,
And the shrine now where mortals are kneeling
  Is a commonplace mart.

Our effeminate fathers and brothers
  Keep carefully out of life's storm,
From the ladylike minds of our mothers
  We are taught that to feel is "bad form."
Our worshipers now and our lovers
  Are calmly devout with their brains,
And we laugh at the man who discovers
  Warm blood in his veins.

But you, O twin souls, passion-mated,
  Who love as the gods loved of old,
What blundering destiny fated

Your lives to be cast in this mold?
Like a lurid volcanic upheaval,
  In pastures prosaic and gray,
You seem with your fervors primeval,
  Among us to-day.

You dropped from some planet of splendor,
  Perhaps as it circled afar,
And your constancy, swerveless and tender,
  You learned from the course of that star.
Fly back to its bosom, I warn you—
  As back to the ark flew the dove—
The minions of earth will but scorn you,
  Because you can love.

THE SEA-BREEZE AND THE SCARF.

HUNG on the casement that looked o'er the main,
  Fluttered a scarf of blue;
And a gay, bold breeze paused to flatter and tease
  This trifle of delicate hue.
"You are lovelier far than the proud skies are,"
  He said with a voice that sighed;
"You are fairer to me than the beautiful sea,
  Oh, why do you stay here and hide?

"You are wasting your life in that dull, dark room
  (And he fondled her silken folds),
O'er the casement lean but a little, my Queen,
  And see what the great world holds.
How the wonderful blue of your matchless hue,
  Cheapens both sea and sky—
You are far too bright to be hidden from sight,
  Come, fly with me, darling—fly."

Tender his whisper and sweet his caress,
  Flattered and pleased was she,
The arms of her lover lifted her over
  The casement out to sea.
Close to his breast she was fondly pressed,
  Kissed once by his laughing mouth;
Then dropped to her grave in the cruel wave
  While the wind went whistling south.

THREE AND ONE.

SOMETIMES she seems so helpless and so mild,
　So full of sweet unreason and so weak,
　So prone to some capricious whim or freak;
Now gay, now tearful, and now anger-wild,
By her strange moods of waywardness beguiled
　And entertained, I stroke her pretty cheek,
　And soothing words of peace and comfort speak;
And love her as a father loves a child.

Sometimes when I am troubled and sore pressed
　On every side by fast advancing care,
　She rises up with such majestic air,
I deem her some Olympian goddess-guest,
Who brings my heart new courage, hope, and rest;
　In her brave eyes dwells balm for my despair,
　And then I seem, while fondly gazing there,
A loving child upon my mother's breast.

Again, when her warm veins are full of life,
   And youth's volcanic tidal wave of fire
   Sends the swift mercury of her pulses higher,
Her beauty stirs my heart to maddening strife,
And all the tiger in my blood is rife;
   I love her with a lover's fierce desire,
   And find in her my dream, complete, entire,
Child, Mother, Mistress—all in one word—Wife.

INBORN.

As long as men have eyes wherewith to gaze,
　　As long as men have eyes.
The sight of beauty to their sense shall be
As mighty winds are to a sleeping sea
　　When stormy billows rise.
And beauty's smile shall stir youth's ardent blood
As rays of sunlight burst the swelling bud;
　　As long as men have eyes wherewith to gaze.

As long as men have words wherewith to praise,
　　As long as men have words,
They shall describe the softly-moulded breast,
Where Love and Pleasure make their downy nest,
　　Like little singing birds;
And lovely limbs, and lips of luscious fire,
Shall be the theme of many a poet's lyre,
　　As long as men have words wherewith to
　　praise.

As long as men have hearts that long for homes,
    As long as men have hearts,
Hid often like the acorn in the earth,
Their inborn love of noble woman's worth,
    Beyond all beauty's arts,
Shall stem the sensuous current of desire,
And urge the world's best thought to something
    higher.
    As long as men have hearts that long for
    homes.

TWO PRAYERS.

HIS.

D EAR, when you lift your gentle heart in prayer,
     Ask God to send His angel Death to me
   Long ere he comes to you, if that may be.
I would dwell with you in that new life there,
     But having, man-like, sinned, I must prepare,
     By sad probation, ere I hope to see
     Those upper realms which are at once thrown free
     To sweet, white souls like yours, unstained and fair
Time is so brief on earth, I well might spare
     A few short years, if so I could atone
     For my marred past, ere you are called above.
My soul would glory in its own despair,
     Till purified I met you at God's throne,
     And entered on Eternities of Love.

HERS.

Nay, Love, not so I frame my prayer to God;
   I want you close beside me to the end;
   If it could be, I would have Him send
A similtaneous death, and let one sod
   Cover our two hushed hearts.   If you have trod
   Paths strange to me on earth, oh, let me wend
   My way with yours hereafter: let me blend
   My tears with yours beneath the chastening rod.
If you must pay the penalty for sin,
   In vales of darkness, ere you pass on higher,
   I will petition God to let me go.
I would not wait on earth, nor enter in
   To any joys before you.   I desire
No glory greater than to share your woe.

SLEEP AND DEATH.

WHEN sleep drops down beside my Love and
    me,
  Although she wears the countenance of a friend,
  A jealous foe we prove her in the end.
In separate barques far out on dreamland's sea,
She lures our wedded souls. Wild winds blow free,
  And drift us wide apart by tides that tend
Tow'rd unknown worlds. Not once our strange
    ways blend
Through the long night, while Sleep looks on in glee.

O Death! be kinder than thy sister seems,
  When at thy call we journey forth some day,
  Through that mysterious and unatlased strait,
To lands more distant than the land of dreams;
  Close, close together let our spirits stay,
  Or else, with one swift stroke annihilate!

ABSENCE.

AFTER you went away, our lovely room
Seemed like a casket whence the soul had fled.
I stood in awful and appalling gloom,
The world was empty and all joy seemed dead.

I think I felt as one might feel who knew
That Death had left him on the earth alone.
For "all the world" to my fond heart means you:
And there is nothing left when you are gone.

Each way I turned my sad, tear-blinded gaze,
I found fresh torture to augment my grief;
Some new reminder of the perfect days
We passed together, beautiful as brief.

There lay a pleasing book that we had read—
And there your latest gift; and everywhere
Some tender act, some loving word you said,
Seemed to take form and mock at my despair.

All happiness that human heart may know
  I find with you; and when you go away,
Those hours become a winding-sheet of woe,
  And make a ghastly phantom of To-day.

LOVE MUCH.

LOVE much.   Earth has enough of bitter in it.
   Cast sweets into its cup whene'er you can.
No heart so hard, but love at last may win it.
   Love is the grand primeval cause of man.
   All hate is foreign to the first great plan.

Love much.   Your heart will be led out to slaughter,
   On altars built of envy and deceit.
Love on, love on! 'tis bread upon the water;
   It shall be cast in loaves yet at your feet,
   Unleavened manna, most divinely sweet.

Love much.   Your faith will be dethroned and
     shaken,
   Your trust betrayed by many a fair, false lure.
Remount your faith, and let new trusts awaken.
   Though clouds obscure them, yet the stars are
     pure;
   Love is a vital force and must endure.

Love much. Mens' souls contract with cold sus-
    picion:
  Shine on them with warm love, and they expand.
'Tis love, not creeds, that from a low condition
  Leads mankind up to heights supreme and grand.
  Oh, that the world could see and understand!

Love much. There is no waste in freely giving;
  More blessed is it, even, than to receive.
He who loves much, alone finds life worth living,
  Love on, through doubt and darkness; and believe
  There is no thing which Love may not achieve.

ONE OF US TWO.

THE day will dawn, when one of us shall hearken
  In vain to hear a voice that has grown dumb.
And morns will fade, noons pale, and shadows
    darken,
  While sad eyes watch for feet that never come.

One of us two must sometime face existence
  Alone with memories that but sharpen pain.
And these sweet days shall shine back in the dis-
    tance,
  Like dreams of summer dawns, in nights of rain.

One of us two, with tortured heart half broken,
  Shall read long-treasured letters through salt tears,
Shall kiss with anguished lips each cherished token,
  That speaks of these loved-crowned, delicious
    years.

One of us two shall find all light, all beauty,
  All joy on earth, a tale forever done;
Shall know henceforth that life means only duty.
  Oh, God! Oh, God! have pity on that one.

HER REVERIE.

WE were both of us—aye, we were both of us
there,
In the self-same house at the play together,
To her it was summer, with bees in the air—
To me it was winter weather.

We never had met, and yet we two
Had played in desperate woman fashion,
A game of life, with a prize in view,
And oh! I played with passion.

'Twas a game that meant heaven and sweet home-life
For the one who went forth with a crown upon
her;
For the one who lost—it meant lone strife,
Sorrow, despair and dishonor,

Well, she won (yet it was not she—
I am told that she was a praying woman:
No earthly power could outwit me—
But hers was superhuman).

She has the prize, and I have—well,
  Memories sweeter than joys of heaven;
Memories fierce as the fires of hell—
  Those unto me were given.

And we sat in the self-same house last night;
  And he was there.   It is no error
When I say (and it gave me keen delight)
  That his eye met mine with terror.

When the love we have won at any cost
  Has grown familiar as some old story,
Naught seems so dear as the love we lost,
  All bright with the Past's weird glory.

And tho' he is fond of that woman, I know—
  I saw in his eyes the brief confession—
That the love seemed sweeter which he let go
  Than that in his possession.

So I am content.   It would be the same
   Were I the wife love-crowned and petted,
And she the woman who lost the game—
   Then she were the one regretted.

And loving him so, I would rather be
   The one he let go—and then vaguely desired,
Than, winning him, once in his face to see
   The look of a love grown tired.

TWO SINNERS.

THERE was a man, it was said one time,
　　Who went astray in his youthful prime.
Can the brain keep cool and the heart keep quiet
When the blood is a river that's running riot?
And boys will be boys the old folks say,
And the man is the better who's had his day.

The sinner reformed; and the preacher told
Of the prodigal son who came back to the fold.
And Christian people threw open the door,
With a warmer welcome than ever before.
Wealth and honor were his to command,
And a spotless woman gave him her hand.

And the world strewed their pathway with blossoms
　　aboom,
Crying "God bless ladye, and God bless groom!"

There was a maiden who went astray
In the golden dawn of her life's young day.
She had more passion and heart than head,
And she followed blindly where fond Love led.
And Love unchecked is a dangerous guide
To wander at will by a fair girl's side.

The woman repented and turned from sin,
But no door opened to let her in.
The preacher prayed that she might be forgiven,
But told her to look for mercy—in Heaven.
For this is the law of the earth, we know:
That the woman is stoned, while the man may go.

A brave man wedded her after all,
But the world said, frowning, "We shall not call."

WHAT LOVE IS.

L OVE is the center and circumference;
    The cause and aim of all things—'tis the key
To joy and sorrow, and the recompense
    For all the ills that have been, or may be.

Love is as bitter as the dregs of sin,
    As sweet as clover-honey in its cell;
Love is the password whereby souls get in
    To Heaven—the gate that leads, sometimes, to
        Hell.

Love is the crown that glorifies; the curse
    That brands and burdens; it is life and death.
It is the great law of the universe;
    And nothing can exist without its breath.

Love is the impulse which directs the world,
    And all things know it and obey its power.
Man, in the maelstrom of his passions whirled;
    The bee that takes the pollen to the flower.

The earth, uplifting her bare, pulsing breast
   To fervent kisses of the amorous sun;—
Each but obeys creative Love's behest,
   Which everywhere instinctively is done.

Love is the only thing that pays for birth,
   Or makes death welcome.　Oh, dear God above
This beautiful but sad, perplexing earth,
   Pity the hearts that know—or know not—Love!

CONSTANCY.

I WILL be true.   Mad stars forsake their courses,
    And led by reckless meteors, turn away
From paths appointed by Eternal Forces;
    But my fixed heart shall never go astray.
Like those calm worlds whose sun-directed motion
    Is undisturbed by strife of wind or sea,
So shall my swerveless and serene devotion
    Sweep on forever, loyal unto thee.

I will be true.   The fickle tide, divided
    Between two wooing shores, in wild unrest
May to and fro shift always undecided;
    Not so the tide of Passion in my breast.
With the grand surge of some resistless river,
    That hurries on, past mountain, vale, and sea,
Unto the main, its waters to deliver,
    So my full heart keeps all its wealth for thee.

4

I will be true.   Light barques may be belated,
   Or turned aside by every breeze at play,
While sturdy ships, well-manned and richly freighted,
   With fair sales flying, anchor safe in Bay,
Like some firm rock, that, steadfast and unshaken,
   Stands all unmoved when ebbing billows flee,
So would my heart stand, faithful if forsaken—
   I will be true, though thou art false to me.

PHILOSOPHICAL.

RESOLVE.

AS the dead year is clasped by a dead December,
  So let your dead sins with your dead days lie.
A new life is yours, and a new hope. Remember,
  We build our own ladders to climb to the sky.
Stand out in the sunlight of Promise, forgetting
  Whatever the Past held of sorrow or wrong.
We waste half our strength in a useless regretting;
  We sit by old tombs in the dark too long.

Have you missed in your aim? Well, the mark is still
    shining.
  Did you faint in the race? Well, take breath for the
    next.
Did the clouds drive you back? But see yonder their
    lining.
  Were you tempted and fell? Let it serve for a text.
As each year hurries by let it join that procession

Of skeleton shapes that march down to the Past,
While you take your place in the line of Progression,
  With your eyes on the heavens, your face to the
    blast.

I tell you the future can hold no terrors
  For any sad soul while the stars revolve,
If he will stand firm on the grave of his errors,
  And instead of regretting, resolve, resolve.
It is never too late to begin rebuilding,
  Though all into ruins your life seems hurled,
For see how the light of the New Year is gilding
  The wan, worn face of the bruised old world.

OPTIMISM.

I'M no reformer; for I see more light
    Than darkness in the world; mine eyes are quick
To catch the first dim radiance of the dawn,
And slow to note the cloud that threatens storm.
The fragrance and the beauty of the rose
Delight me so, slight thought I give its thorn;
And the sweet music of the lark's clear song
Stays longer with me than the night hawk's cry.
And e'en in this great throe of pain called Life
I find a rapture linked with each despair,
Well worth the price of anguish.   I detect
More good than evil in humanity.
Love lights more fires than hate extinguishes,
And men grow better as the world grows old.

PAIN'S PROOF.

I THINK man's great capacity for pain
    Proves his immortal birthright.   I am sure
No merely human mind could bear the strain
    Of some tremendous sorrows we endure.

Art's most ingenious breastworks fail at length
    Beat by the mighty billows of the sea;
Only the God-formed shores possess the strength
    To stand before their onslaughts, and not flee.

The structure that we build with careful toil,
    The tempest lays in ruins in an hour;
While some grand tree that springs forth from the soil
    Is bended but not broken by its power.

Unless our souls had root in soil divine
    We could not bear earth's overwhelming strife.
The fiercest pain that racks this heart of mine,
    Convinces me of everlasting life.

IMMORTALITY.

IMMORTAL life is something to be earned,
By slow self-conquest, comradeship with Pain,
And patient seeking after higher truths.
We cannot follow our own wayward wills,
And feed our baser appetites, and give
Loose rein to foolish tempers year on year,
And then cry, " Lord forgive me, I believe."
And straightway bathe in glory. Men must learn
God's system is too grand a thing for that.
The spark divine dwells in our souls, and we
Can fan it to a steady flame of light,
Whose luster gilds the pathway to the tomb,
And shines on through Eternity, or else
Neglect it till it glimmers down to Death,
And leaves us but the darkness of the grave.
Each conquered passion feeds the living flame;
Each well-born sorrow is a step towards God;
Faith cannot rescue, and no blood redeem

The soul that will not reason and resolve.
Lean on thyself, yet prop thyself with prayer,
(All hope is prayer; who calls it hope no more,
Sends prayer footsore forth over weary wastes,
While he who calls it prayer gives wings to hope,)
And there are spirits, messengers of Love,
Who come at call and fortify our strength.
Make friends with them, and with thine inner self;
Cast out all envy, bitterness, and hate;
And keep the mind's fair tabernacle pure.
Shake hands with Pain, give greeting unto Grief,
Those angels in disguise, and thy glad soul
From height to height, from star to shining star,
Shall climb and claim blest immortality.

ANSWERED PRAYERS.

I PRAYED for riches, and achieved success;
  All that I touched turned into gold. Alas!
My cares were greater and my peace was less,
  When that wish came to pass.

I prayed for glory, and I heard my name
  Sung by sweet children and by hoary men.
But ah! the hurts—the hurts that come with fame!
  I was not happy then.

I prayed for Love, and had my heart's desire.
  Through quivering heart and body, and through
    brain
There swept the flame of its devouring fire,
  And but the scars remain.

I prayed for a contented mind. At length
  Great light upon my darkened spirit burst.
Great peace fell on me also, and great strength—
  Oh, had that prayer been first!

THE LADY OF TEARS.

THROUGH valley and hamlet and city,
　　Wherever humanity dwells,
With a heart full of infinite pity,
　　A breast that with sympathy swells,
She walks in her beauty immortal.
　　Each household grows sad as she nears,
But she crosses at length every portal,
　　The mystical Lady of Tears.

If never this vision of sorrow
　　Has shadowed your life in the past,
You will meet her, I know, some to-morrow—
　　She visits all hearthstones at last.
To hovel, and cottage, and palace,
　　To servant and king she appears,
And offers the gall of her chalice—
　　The unwelcome Lady of Tears.

To the eyes that have smiled but in gladness,
    To the souls that have basked in the sun,
She seems in her garments of sadness,
    A creature to dread and to shun.
And lips that have drank but of pleasure
    Grow pallid and tremble with fears,
As she portions the gall from her measure,
    The merciless Lady of Tears.

But in midnight, lone hearts that are quaking,
    With the agonized numbness of grief,
Are saved from the torture of breaking,
    By her bitter-sweet draught of relief.
Oh, then do all graces enfold her;
    Like a goddess she looks and appears,
And the eyes overflow that behold her—
    The beautiful Lady of Tears.

Though she turns to lamenting, all laughter,
　　Though she gives us despair for delight,
Life holds a new meaning thereafter,
　　For those who will greet her aright.
They stretch out their hands to each other,
　　For Sorrow unites and endears,
The children of one tender mother
　　The sweet, blessed Lady of Tears.

THE MASTER HAND.

IT is something too strange to understand,
  How all the chords on the instrument,
Whether sorrowful, blithe, or grand,
Under the touch of your master hand
  Were into one melody blent.
Major, minor, everything—all—
Came at your magic fingers' call.

Why! famed musicians had turned in despair
  Again and again from those self-same keys;
They mayhap brought forth a simple air,
But a discord always crept in somewhere,
  In their fondest efforts to please.
Or a jarring, jangling, meaningless strain
Angered the silence to noisy pain.

"Out of tune," they would frown and say;
  Or "a loosened key" or "a broken string;"

But sure and certain they were alway,
That no man living on earth could play
　　Measures more perfect, or bring
Sweeter sounds or a truer air
Out of that curious instrument there.

And then you came.　You swept the scale
　　With a mighty master's wonderful art.
You made the minor keys sob and wail,
While the low notes rang like a bell in a gale.
　　And every chord in my heart,
From the deep bass tones to the shrill ones above,
Joined into that glorious harmony—Love.

And now, though I live for a thousand years,
　　On no new chord can a new hand fall.
The chords of sorrow, of pain, of tears,
The chords of raptures and hopes and fears,
　　I say you have struck them all;
And all the meaning put into each strain
By the Great Composer, you have made plain.

SECRET THOUGHTS.

I HOLD it true that thoughts are things
    Endowed with bodies, breath, and wings,
And that we send them forth to fill
The world with good results—or ill.

That which we call our secret thought
Speeds to the earth's remotest spot,
And leaves its blessings or its woes
Like tracks behind it as it goes.

It is God's law.   Remember it
In your still chamber as you sit
With thoughts you would not dare have known,
And yet make comrades when alone.

These thoughts have life; and they will fly
And leave their impress by-and-by,
Like some marsh breeze, whose poisoned breath
Breathes into homes its fevered breath.

5

And after you have quite forgot
Or all outgrown some vanished thought,
Back to your mind to make its home,
A dove or raven, it will come.

Then let your secret thoughts be fair;
They have a vital part and share
In shaping worlds and molding fate—
God's system is so intricate.

THERE COMES A TIME.

THERE comes a time to every mortal being,
  Whate'er his station or his lot in life,
When his sad soul yearns for the final freeing
  From all this jarring and unceasing strife.

There comes a time, when, having lost its savor,
  The salt of wealth is worthless; when the mind
Grows wearied with the world's capricious favor,
  And sighs for something that it cannot find.

There comes a time, when, though kind friends are
    thronging
  About our pathway with sweet acts of grace,
We feel a vast and overwhelming longing
  For something that we cannot name or place.

There comes a time, when, with earth's best love by us,
  To feed the heart's great hunger and desire,
We find not even this can satisfy us;
  The soul within us cries for something higher.

What greater proof need we that we inherit
  A life immortal in another sphere?
It is the homesick longing of the spirit
  That cannot find its satisfaction here.

THE WORLD.

WITH noiseless steps good goes its way;
    The earth shakes under evil's tread.
  We hear the uproar, and 'tis said,
The world grows wicked every day.

It is not true. With quiet feet,
  In silence, Virtue sows her seeds;
  While Sin goes shouting out his deeds,
And echoes listen and repeat.

But surely as the old world moves,
  And circles round the shining sun,
  So surely does God's purpose run,
And all the human race improves.

Despite bold evil's noise and stir,
  Truth's golden harvests ripen fast;
  The Present far outshines the Past;
Men's thoughts are higher than they were.

Who runs may read this truth, I say:
　Sin travels in a rumbling car,
　While Virtue soars on like a star—
The world grows better every day.

NECESSITY.

NECESSITY, whom long I deemed my foe,
  Thou cold, unsmiling, and hard-visaged dame,
Now I no longer see thy face, I know
  Thou wert my friend beyond reproach or blame.

My best achievements and the fairest flights
  Of my winged fancy were inspired by thee;
Thy stern voice stirred me to the mountain heights;
  Thy importunings bade me do and be.

But for thy breath, the spark of living fire
  Within me might have smoldered out at length;
But for thy lash which would not let me tire,
  I never would have measured my own strength.

But for thine ofttimes merciless control
  Upon my life, that nerved me past despair,
I never should have dug deep in my soul
  And found the mine of treasures hidden there.

And though we walk divided pathways now,
  And I no more may see thee, to the end,
I weave this little chaplet for thy brow,
  That other hearts may know, and hail thee friend.

ACHIEVEMENT.

TRUST in thine own untried capacity
    As thou wouldst trust in God Himself. Thy
        soul
Is but an emanation from the whole.
Thou dost not dream what forces lie in thee,
Vast and unfathomed as the grandest sea.
    Thy silent mind o'er diamond caves may roll,
    Go seek them—but let pilot will control
Those passions which thy favoring winds can be.

No man shall place a limit in thy strength;
    Such triumphs as no mortal ever gained
    May yet be thine if thou wilt but believe
In thy Creator and thyself. At length
    Some feet will tread all heights now unattained—
    Why not thine own? Press on; achieve! achieve!

BELIEF.

THE pain we have to suffer seems so broad,
　　Set side by side with this life's narrow span,
We need no greater evidence that God
　　Has some diviner destiny for man.

He would not deem it worth His while to send
　　Such crushing sorrows as pursue us here,
Unless beyond this fleeting journey's end
　　Our chastened spirits found another sphere.

So small this world! So vast its agonies!
　　A future life is needed to adjust
These ill-proportioned, wide discrepancies
　　Between the spirit and its frame of dust.

So when my soul writhes with some aching grief,
　　And all my heart-strings tremble at the strain,
My Reason lends new courage to Belief,
　　And all God's hidden purposes seem plain.

WHATEVER IS — IS BEST.

I KNOW as my life grows older,
  And mine eyes have clearer sight—
That under each rank wrong, somewhere
  There lies the root of Right;
That each sorrow has its purpose,
  By the sorrowing oft unguessed,
But as sure as the sun brings morning,
  Whatever is—is best.

I know that each sinful action,
  As sure as the night brings shade,
Is somewhere, sometime punished,
  Tho' the hour be long delayed.
I know that the soul is aided
  Sometimes by the heart's unrest,
And to grow means often to suffer—
  But whatever is—is best.

I know there are no errors,
   In the great Eternal plan,
And all things work together
   For the final good of man.
And I know when my soul speeds onward,
   In its grand Eternal quest,
I shall say as I look back earthward,
   Whatever is—is best.

PEACE AT THE GOAL.

FROM the soul of a man who was homeless
    Came the deathless song of home.
And the praises of rest are chanted best
    By those who are forced to roam.

In a time of fast and hunger,
    We can talk over feasts divine;
But the banquet done, why, where is the one
    Who can tell you the taste of the wine?

We think of the mountain's grandeur
    As we walk in the heat afar—
But when we sit in the shadows of it
    We think how at rest we are.

With the voice of the craving passions
    We can picture a love to come.
But the heart once filled, lo, the voice is stilled,
    And we stand in the silence—dumb.

THE LAW.

LIFE is a Shylock; always it demands
   The fullest usurer's interest for each pleasure.
Gifts are not freely scattered by its hands;
We make returns for every borrowed treasure.

Each talent, each achievement, and each gain
Necessitates some penalty to pay.
Delight imposes lassitude and pain,
As certainly as darkness follows day.

All you bestow on causes or on men,
Of love or hate, of malice or devotion,
Somehow, sometime, shall be returned again—
There is no wasted toil, no lost emotion.

The motto of the world is give and take.
It gives you favors—out of sheer goodwill.
But unless speedy recompense you make,
You'll find yourself presented with its bill.

When rapture comes to thrill the heart of you,
Take it with tempered gratitude.　Remember,
Some later time the interest will fall due.
No year brings June that does not bring December.

RECOMPENSE.

STRAIGHT through my heart this fact to-day,
    By Truth's own hand is driven:
God never takes one thing away,
    But something else is given.

I did not know in earlier years,
    This law of love and kindness;
I only mourned through bitter tears
    My loss, in sorrow's blindness.

But, ever following each regret
    O'er some departed treasure,
My sad repining heart was met
    With unexpected pleasure.

I thought it only happened so;
    But Time this truth has taught me—
No least thing from my life can go,
    But something else is brought me.

It is the Law, complete, sublime;
   And now with Faith unshaken,
In patience I but bide my time,
   When any joy is taken.

No matter if the crushing blow
   May for the moment down me,
Still, back of it waits Love, I know,
   With some new gift to crown me.

6

DESIRE.

NO joy for which thy hungering heart has panted,
      No hope it cherishes through waiting years,
But if thou dost deserve it, shall be granted
For with each passionate wish the blessing nears.

Tune up the fine, strong instrument of thy being
To chord with thy dear hope, and do not tire.
When both in key and rhythm are agreeing,
Lo! thou shalt kiss the lips of thy desire.

The thing thou cravest so waits in the distance,
Wrapt in the silences, unseen and dumb:
Essential to thy soul and thy existence—
Live worthy of it—call, and it shall come.

DEATHLESS.

THERE lies in the center of each man's heart,
 A longing and love for the good and pure;
And if but an atom, or larger part,
 I tell you this shall endure—endure
After the body has gone to decay—
 Yea, after the world has passed away.

The longer I live and the more I see
 Of the struggle of souls toward the heights above,
The stronger this truth comes home to me:
 That the Universe rests on the shoulders of love;
A love so limitless, deep, and broad,
 That men have renamed it and called it—God.

And nothing that ever was born or evolved,
 Nothing created by light or force,
But deep in its system there lies dissolved
 A shining drop from the Great Love Source;
A shining drop that shall live for aye—
 Though kingdoms may perish and stars decay.

KEEP OUT OF THE PAST.

KEEP out of the Past! for its highways
    Are damp with malarial gloom;
Its gardens are sere and its forests are drear,
    And everywhere molders a tomb.
Who seeks to regain its lost pleasures,
    Finds only a rose turned to dust;
And its storehouse of wonderful treasures
    Are covered and coated with rust.

Keep out of the Past.   It is haunted:
    He who in its avenues gropes,
Shall find there the ghost of a joy prized the most,
    And a skeleton throng of dead hopes.
In place of its beautiful rivers,
    Are pools that are stagnant with slime;
And these graves gleaming in a phosphoric light,
    Hide dreams that were slain in their prime.

Keep out of the Past.   It is lonely,
  And barren and bleak to the view;
Its fires have grown cold, and its stories are old—
  Turn, turn to the Present—the New:
To-day leads you up to the hilltops
  That are kissed by the radiant sun,
To-day shows no tomb, life's hopes are in bloom,
  And to-day holds a prize to be won.

THE FAULT OF THE AGE.

THE fault of the age is a mad endeavor
　　To leap to heights that were made to climb:
By a burst of strength, of a thought most clever,
　　We plan to forestall and outwit Time.

We scorn to wait for the thing worth having;
　　We want high noon at the day's dim dawn;
We find no pleasure in toiling and saving,
　　As our forefathers did in the old times gone.

We force our roses, before their season,
　　To bloom and blossom for us to wear;
And then we wonder and ask the reason
　　Why perfect buds are so few and rare.

We crave the gain, but despise the getting;
　　We want wealth—not as reward, but dower;
And the strength that is wasted in useless fretting
　　Would fell a forest or build a tower.

· To covet the prize, yet to shrink from the winning;
   To thirst for glory, yet fear to fight;
Why what can it lead to at last but sinning,
   To mental languor and moral blight?

Better the old slow way of striving,
   And counting small gains when the year is done,
Than to use our force and our strength in contriving,
   And to grasp for pleasure we have not won.

DISTRUST.

DISTRUST that man who tells you to distrust;
　　He takes the measure of his own small soul,
And thinks the world no larger.　He who prates
Of human nature's baseness and deceit
Looks in the mirror of his heart, and sees
His kind therein reflected.　Or perchance
The honeyed wine of life was turned to gall
By sorrow's hand, which brimmed his cup with tears,
And made all things seem bitter to his taste.
Give him compassion!　But be not afraid
Of nectared Love, or Friendship's strengthening
　　draught,
Nor think a poison underlies their sweets.
Look through true eyes—you will discover truth;
Suspect suspicion, and doubt only doubt.

ARTIST AND MAN.

TAKE thy life better than thy work. Too oft
　　Our artists spend their skill in rounding soft
Fair curves upon their statues, while the rough
And ragged edges of the unhewn stuff
In their own natures startle and offend
The eye of critic and the heart of friend.

If in thy too brief day thou must neglect
Thy labor or thy life, let men detect
Flaws in thy work! while their most searching gaze
Can fall on nothing which they may not praise
In thy well chiseled character.   The Man
Should not be shadowed by the Artisan!

MISCELLANEOUS.

BABYLAND.

HAVE you heard of the Valley of Babyland,
  The realm where the dear little darlings stay,
Till the kind storks go, as all men know,
  And, oh, so tenderly bring them away?
The paths are winding and past all finding,
  By all save the storks who understand
The gates and the highways and the intricate byways
                    That lead to Babyland.

All over the Valley of Babyland
  Sweet flowers bloom in the soft green moss;
And under the ferns fair, and under the plants there,
  Lie little heads like spools of floss.
With a soothing number the river of slumber
  Flows o'er a bedway of silver sand;
And angels are keeping watch o'er the sleeping
                    Babes of Babyland.

The path to the Valley of Babyland
  Only the kingly, kind storks know;
If they fly over mountains, or wade through fount-
    ains.
  No man sees them come or go.
But an angel maybe, who guards some baby,
  Or a fairy perhaps, with her magic wand,
Brings them straightway to the wonderful gateway
              That leads to Babyland.

And there in the Valley of Babyland,
  Under the mosses and leaves and ferns,
Like an unfledged starling, they find the darling,
  For whom the heart of a mother yearns;
And they lift him lightly, and snug him tightly
  In feathers soft as a lady's hand;
And off with a rockaway step they walk away
              Out of Babyland.

As they go from the Valley of Babyland,
  Forth into the world of great unrest,

Sometimes in weeping, he wakes from sleeping
  Before he reaches the mother's breast.
Ah, how she blesses him, how she caresses him,
  Bonniest bird in the bright home band
That o'er land and water, the kind stork brought her
                      From far off Babyland.

A FACE.

BETWEEN the curtains of snowy lace,
　　Over the way is a baby's face;
It peeps forth, smiling in merry glee,
　　And waves its pink little hand at me.

My heart responds with a lonely cry—
　　But in the wonderful By-and-By—
Out from the window of God's "To Be,"
　　That other baby shall beckon to me.

That ever haunting and longed-for face,
　　That perfect vision of infant grace,
Shall shine on me in a splendor of light,
　　Never to fade from my eager sight.

All that was taken shall be made good;
　　All that puzzles me understood;
And the wee white hand that I lost, one day,
　　Shall lead me into the Better Way.

AN OLD COMRADE.

ALL suddenly between me and the light,
   That brightly shone, and warm,
Robed in the pall-like garments of the night,
   There rose a shadowy form.

"Stand back," I said; "you quite obscure the sun;
   What do you want with me?"
"Dost thou not know, then?" quoth the mystic one;
   "Look on my face and see!"

I looked, and, lo! it was my old despair,
   Robed in a new disguise;
In blacker garments than it used to wear,
   But with the same sad eyes.

So ghostly were the memories it awoke,
   I shrank in fear away.
"Nay, be more kind," 'twas thus the dark shape
     spoke,
   "For I have come to stay.

7

"So long thy feet have trod on sunny heights,
  Such joys thy heart has known,
Perchance thou hast forgotten those long nights,
  When we two watched alone,

"Though sweet and dear the pleasures thou hast met,
  And comely to thine eye,
Has one of them, in all that bright throng yet,
  Been half so true as I?

"And that last rapture which ensnared thee so
  With pleasure twin to pain,
It was the swiftest of them all to go—
  But I—I will remain.

"Again we two will live a thousand years,
  In desperate nights of grief,
That shall refuse the bitter balm of tears,
  For thy bruised heart's relief.

"Again we two will watch the hopeless dawn
　　Creep up a lonely sky—
Again we'll urge the drear day to be gone,
　　Yet dread to see it die.

"Nay, shrink not from me, for I am thy friend,
　　One whom the Master sent;
And I shall help thee, ere we reach the end,
　　To find a great content.

"And I will give thee courage to attain,
　　The heights supremely fair,
Wherein thou'lt cry, 'How blessed was my pain!
　　How God sent my Despair!' "

ENTRE-ACTE REVERIES.

BETWEEN the acts while the orchestra played
    That sweet old waltz with the lilting measure,
I drifted away to a dear dead day,
    When the dance, for me, was the sum of all
      pleasure;
When my veins were rife with the fever of life,
    When hope ran high as an inswept ocean,
And my heart's great gladness was almost madness,
    As I floated off to the music's motion.

How little I cared for the world outside!
    How little I cared for the dull day after!
The thought of trouble went up like a bubble,
    And burst in a sparkle of mirthful laughter.
Oh! and the beat of it, oh! and the sweet of it-
    Melody, motion, and young blood melted;
The dancers swaying, the players playing,
    The air song-deluged and music-pelted.

I knew no weariness, no, not I—
  My step was as light as the waving grasses
That flutter with ease on the strong-armed breeze,
  As it waltzes over the wild morasses.
Life was all sound and swing; youth was a perfect
    thing;
  Night was the goddess of satisfaction.
Oh, how I tripped away, right to the edge of day!
  Joy lay in motion, and rest lay in action.

I dance no more on the music's wave,
  I yield no more to its wildering power,
That time has flown like a rose that is blown,
  Yet life is a garden forever in flower.
Though storms of tears have watered the years,
  Between to-day and the day departed,
Though trials have met me, and grief's waves wet me,
  And I have been tired and trouble-hearted.

Though under the sod of a wee green grave,
  A great, sweet hope in darkness perished,

Yet life, to my thinking, is a cup worth drinking,
    A gift to be glad of, and loved, and cherished.
There is deeper pleasure in the slower measure
    That Time's grand orchestra now is playing.
Its mellowed minor is sadder but finer,
    And life grows daily more worth the living.

A PLEA.

COLUMBIA, large-hearted and tender,
  Too long for the good of your kin
You have shared your home's comfort and splendor
  With all who have asked to come in.
The smile of your true eyes has lighted
  The way to your wide-open door.
You have held out full hands, and invited
  The beggar to take from your store.

Your overrun proud sister nations,
  Whose offspring you help them to keep,
Are sending their poorest relations,
  Their unruly vicious black sheep;
Unwashed and unlettered you take them,
  And lo! we are pushed from your knee;
We are governed by laws as they make them,
  We are slaves in the land of the free.

Columbia, you know the devotion
  Of those who have sprung from your soil;
Shall aliens, born over the ocean,
  Dispute us the fruits of our toil?
Most noble and gracious of mothers,
  Your children rise up and demand
That you bring us no more foster brothers,
  To breed discontent in the land.

Be prudent before you are zealous,
  Not generous only—but just.
Our hearts are grown wrathful and jealous
  Toward those who have outraged your trust.
They jostle and crowd in our places,
  They sneer at the comforts you gave.
We say, shut the door in their faces—
  Until they have learned to behave!

In hearts that are greedy and hateful,
  They harbor ill-will and deceit;

They ask for more favors, ungrateful
  For those you have poured at their feet.
Rise up in your grandeur, and straightway
  Bar out the bold, clamoring mass;
Let sentinels stand at your gateway,
  To see who is worthy to pass.

Give first to your own faithful toilers
  The freedom our birthright should claim,
And take from these ruthless despoilers
  The power which they use to our shame.
Columbia, too long you have dallied
  With foes whom you feed from your store;
It is time that your wardens were rallied,
  And stationed outside the locked door.

THE ROOM BENEATH THE RAFTERS.

SOMETIMES when I have dropped to sleep,
    Draped in a soft luxurious gloom,
Across my drowsing mind will creep
    The memory of another room,
Where resinous knots in roof boards made
A frescoing of light and shade,
And sighing poplars brushed their leaves
Against the humbly sloping eaves.

Again I fancy, in my dreams,
    I'm lying in my trundle bed;
I seem to see the bare old beams
    And unhewn rafters overhead.
The mud wasp's shrill falsetto hum
I hear again, and see him come
Forth from his dark-walled hanging house,
Dressed in his black and yellow blouse.

There, summer dawns, in sleep I stirred,
 And wove into my fair dream's woof
The chattering of a martin bird,
 Or rain-drops pattering on the roof.
Or half awake, and half in fear,
I saw the spider spinning near
His pretty castle where the fly
Should come to ruin by-and-by.

And there I fashioned from my brain
 Youth's shining structures in the air.
I did not wholly build in vain,
 For some were lasting, firm and fair.
And I am one who lives to say
My life has held more gold than gray,
And that the splendor of the real
Surpassed my early dream's ideal.

But still I love to wander back
 To that old time and that old place;

To tread my way o'er memory's track,
   And catch the early morning grace,
In that quaint room beneath the rafter,
That echoed to my childish laughter;
To dream again the dreams that grew
More beautiful as they came true.

THE MOTHER-IN-LAW.

SHE was my dream's fulfilment and my joy,
    This lovely woman whom you call your wife.
You sported at your play, an idle boy,
    When I first felt the stirring of her life
Within my startled being.   I was thrilled
With such intensity of love, it filled
The very universe! But words are vain—
No man can comprehend that wild, sweet pain.

You smiled in childhood's slumber while I felt
    The agonies of labour; and the nights
I, weeping, o'er the little sufferer knelt,
    You, wandering on through dreamland's fair de-
        lights
Flung out your lengthening limbs and slept and
        grew;
While I, awake, saved this dear wife for you.

She was my heart's loved idle and my pride.
  I taught her all those graces which you praise,
I dreamed of coming years, when at my side
  She should lend luster to my fading days,
Should cling to me (as she to you clings now),
The young fruit hanging to the withered bough.
But lo! the blossom was so fair a sight,
You plucked it from me—for your own delight.

Well, you are worthy of her—oh, thank God—
  And yet I think you do not realize
How burning were the sands o'er which I trod,
  To bear and rear this woman you so prize.
It was no easy thing to see her go—
Even into the arms of the one she worshiped so.

How strong, how vast, how awful seems the power
  Of this new love which fills a maiden's heart,
For one who never bore a single hour
  Of pain for her; which tears her life apart
From all its moorings, and controls her more

Than all the ties the years have held before;
Which crowns a stranger with a kingly grace—
And give the one who bore her—second place!

She loves me still! and yet, were Death to say,
   "Choose now between them!" you would be her
     choice.
God meant it to be so—it is His way.
   But can you wonder if, while I rejoice
In her content, this thought hurts like a knife—
"No longer necessary to her life!"

My pleasure in her joy is bitter sweet.
   Your very goodness sometimes hurts my heart,
Because, for her, life's drama seems complete
   Without the mother's oft-repeated part.
Be patient with me! She was mine so long
Who now is yours. One must indeed be strong,
To meet the loss without the least regret.
And so, forgive me, if my eyes are wet.

AN OLD FAN.

(TO KITTY. HER REVERIE.)

I T is soiled and quite passe,
   Broken too, and out of fashion,
But it stirs my heart some way,
As I hold it here to-day,
With a dead year's grace and passion.
  Oh, my pretty fan!

Precious dream and thrilling strain,
   Rise up from that vanished season;
Back to heart and nerve and brain
Sweeps the joy as keen as pain,
Joy that asks no cause or reason.
  Oh, my dainty fan!

Hopes that perished in a night
   Gaze at me like spectral faces;

Grim despair and lost delight,
Sorrow long since gone from sight—
All are hiding in these laces.
 Oh, my broken fan!

Let us lay the thing away—
 I am sadder now and older;
Fled the ball-room and the play—
You have had your foolish day,
And the night and life are colder.
 Exit—little fan!

NO CLASSES!

NO classes here! Why, that is idle talk.
　　The village beau sneers at the country boor;
The importuning mendicants who walk
　　Our cities' streets despise the parish poor.

The daily toiler at some noisy loom
　　Holds back her garments from the kitchen aid.
Meanwhile the latter leans upon her broom,
　　Unconscious of the bow the laundress made.

The grocer's daughter eyes the farmer's lass
　　With haughty glances; and the lawyer's wife
Would pay no visits to the trading class,
　　If policy were not her creed in life.

The merchant's son nods coldly at the clerk;
　　The proud possessor of a pedigree
Ignores the youth whose father rose by work;
　　The title-seeking maiden scorns all three.

The aristocracy of blood looks down
   Upon the "nouveau riche;" and in disdain,
The lovers of the intellectual frown
   On both, and worship at the shrine of brain.

"No classes here," the clergyman has said;
   "We are one family." Yet see his rage
And horror when his favorite son would wed
   Some pure and pretty player on the stage.

It is the vain but natural human way
   Of vaunting our weak selves, our pride, our worth!
Not till the long-delayed millennial day
   Shall we behold "no classes" on God's earth.

A GRAY MOOD.

AS we hurry away to the end, my friend,
    Of this sad little farce called existence,
We are sure that the future will bring one thing,
    And that is the grave in the distance.
And so when our lives run along all wrong,
    And nothing seems real or certain,
We can comfort ourselves with the thought,(or not)
    Of that specter behind the curtain.

But we haven't much time to repine or whine,
    Or to wound or jostle each other;
And the hour for us each is to-day, I say,
    If we mean to assist a brother.
And there is no pleasure that earth gives birth,
    But the worry it brings is double;
And all that repays for the strife of life,
    Is helping some soul in trouble.

I tell you, if I could go back the track
　　To my life's morning hour,
I would not set forth seeking name or fame,
　　Or that poor bauble called power.
I would be like the sunlight, and live to give;
　　I would lend but I would not borrow;
Nor would I be blind and complain of pain,
　　Forgetting the meaning of sorrow.

This world is a vaporous jest at best,
　　Tossed off by the gods in laughter;
And a cruel attempt at wit were it,
　　If nothing better came after.
It is reeking with hearts that ache and break,
　　Which we ought to comfort and strengthen,
As we hurry away to the end, my friend,
　　And the shadows behind us lengthen.

AT AN OLD DRAWER.

BEFORE this scarf was faded,
    What hours of mirth it knew!
How gaily it paraded
    For smiling eyes to view!
The days were tinged with glory,
    The nights too quickly sped,
And life was like a story
    Where all the people wed.

Before this rosebud wilted,
    How passionately sweet
The wild waltz swelled and lilted
    In time for flying feet!
How loud the bassoons muttered!
    The horns grew madly shrill;
And, oh, the vows lips uttered
    That hearts could not fulfill.

Before this fan was broken,
  Behind its lace and pearl
What whispered words were spoken—
  What hearts were in a whirl!
What homesteads were selected
  In Fancy's realm of Spain!
What castles were erected,
  Without a room for pain!

When this odd glove was mated,
  How thrilling seemed the play!
May be our hearts are sated—
  They tire so soon to-day.
Oh, shut away those treasures,
  They speak the dreary truth—
We have outgrown the pleasures
  And keen delights of youth.

THE OLD STAGE QUEEN.

BACK in the box by the curtains shaded,
    She sits alone by the house unseen;
Her eye is dim, her cheek is faded,
    She who was once the people's queen.

The curtain rolls up, and she sees before her
    A vision of beauty and youth and grace.
Ah! no wonder all hearts adore her,
    Silver-throated and fair of face.

Out of her box she leans and listens;
    Oh, is it with pleasure or with despair
That her thin cheek pales and her dim eye glistens,
    While that fresh young voice sings the grand old
        air?

She is back again in the Past's bright splendor—
    When life seemed worth living, and love a truth,
Ere Time had told her she must surrender
    Her double dower of fame and youth.

It is she herself who stands there singing
　To that sea of faces that shines and stirs;
And the cheers on cheers that go up ringing
　And rousing the echoes—are hers—all hers.

Just for one moment the sweet delusion
　Quickens her pulses and blurs her sight,
And wakes within her that wild confusion
　Of joy that is anguish and fierce delight.

Then the curtain goes down and the lights are
　　gleaming
　Brightly o'er circle and box and stall.
She starts like a sleeper who wakes from dreaming—
　Her past lies under a funeral pall.

Her day is dead and her star descended
　Never to rise or shine again;
Her reign is over—her Queenship ended—
　A new name is sounded and sung by men.

All the glitter and glow and splendor,
 All the glory of that lost day,
With the friends that seemed true, and the love that
  seemed tender,
 Why, what is it all but a dead bouquet?

She rises to go.   Has the night turned colder?
 The new Queen answers to call and shout;
And the old Queen looks back over her shoulder,
 Then all unnoticed she passes out.

FAITH.

I WILL not doubt, though all my ships at sea
   Come drifting home with broken masts and sails;
I shall believe the Hand which never fails,
   From seeming evil worketh good for me;
And though I weep because those sails are battered,
   Still will I cry, while my best hopes lie shattered,
               "I trust in thee."

I will not doubt, though all my prayers return
   Unanswered from the still, white Realm above;
I shall believe it is an all-wise Love
   Which has refused those things for which I yearn;
And though at times I cannot keep from grieving,
   Yet the pure ardor of my fixed believing
               Undimmed shall burn.

I will not doubt, though sorrows fall like rain,
   And troubles swarm like bees about a hive;

I shall believe the heights for which I strive
  Are only reached by anguish and by pain;
And though I groan and tremble with my crosses,
  I yet shall see, through my severest losses,
                The greater gain.

I will not doubt; well anchored in the faith,
  Like some staunch ship, my soul braves every gale,
So strong its courage that it will not fail
  To breast the mighty unknown sea of Death.
Oh, may I cry when body parts with spirit,
  "I do not doubt," so listening worlds may hear it,
                With my last breath.

THE TRUE KNIGHT.

WE sigh above historic pages,
    Brave with the deeds of courtly men,
And wish those peers of middle ages
    In our dull day could live again.
And yet no knight or Troubadour began
In chivalry with the American.

He does not frequent joust or tourney,
    And flaunt his lady's colors there;
But in the tedium of a journey,
    He shows that deferential care—
That thoughtful kindness to the sex at large,
Which makes each woman feel herself his charge.

He does not challenge foes to duel,
    To win his lady's cast-off glove,
But proves in ways less rash and cruel,
    The truth and fervor of his love.

Not by bold deeds, but by his reverent mien,
He pays his public tribute to his Queen.

He may not shine with courtly graces,
   But yet, his kind, respectful air
To woman, whatsoe'er her place is,
   It might be well if kings could share.
So, for the chivalric true gentleman,
Give me, I say, our own American.

THE CITY.

I OWN the charms of lovely Nature; still,
    In human nature more delight I find.
Though sweet the murmuring voices of the rill,
    I much prefer the voices of my kind.

I like the roar of cities.   In the mart,
    Where busy toilers strive for place and gain,
I seem to read humanity's great heart,
    And share its hopes, its pleasures, and its pain.

The rush of hurrying trains that cannot wait,
    The tread of myriad feet, all say to me:
"You are the architect of your own fate;
    Toil on, hope on, and dare to do and be."

I like the jangled music of the loud
    Bold bells; the whistle's sudden shrill reply;
And there is inspiration in a crowd—
    A magnetism flashed from eye to eye.

My sorrows all seem lightened and my joys
    Augmented when the comrade world walks near;
Close to mankind my soul best keeps its poise.
    Give me the great town's bustle, strife, and noise
    And let who will, hold Nature's calm more dear.

WOMAN.

GIVE us that grand word "woman" once again,
　　And let's have done with "lady": one's a term
Full of fine force, strong, beautiful, and firm,
Fit for the noblest use of tongue or pen;
And one's a word for lackeys.　One suggests
The Mother, Wife, and Sister!　One the dame
Whose costly robe, mayhap, gives her the name.
One word upon its own strength leans and rests;
The other minces tiptoe.　Who would be
The perfect woman must grow brave of heart
And broad of soul to play her troubled part
Well in life's drama.　While each day we see
The "perfect lady" skilled in what to do
And what to say, grace in each tone and act
('Tis taught in schools, but needs some native tact),
Yet narrow in her mind as in her shoe.
Give the first place then to the nobler phrase,
And leave the lesser word for lesser praise.

9

THE SOUL'S FAREWELL TO THE BODY.

SO we must part forever; and although
  I long have beat my wings and cried to go,
Free from your narrow limiting control,
Forth into space, the true home of the soul,

Yet now, yet now that hour is drawing near,
I pause reluctant, finding you so dear.
All joys await me in the realm of God—
Must you, my comrade, moulder in the sod?

I was your captive, yet you were my slave:
Your prisoner, yet obedience you gave
To all my earnest wishes and commands.
Now to the worm I leave those willing hands

That toiled for me or held the books I read,
Those feet that trod where'er I wished to tread,
Those arms that clasped my dear ones, and the breast
On which one loved and loving heart found rest,

Those lips through which my prayers to God have
  risen,
Those eyes that were the windows to my prison.
From these, all these, Death's Angel bids me sever;
Dear Comrade Body, fare thee well forever!

I go to my inheritance, and go
With joy that only the freed soul can know;
Yet in my spirit wanderings I trust
I may sometimes pause near your sacred dust.

THIMBLE ISLANDS.

(OFF LONG ISLAND SOUND.)

BETWEEN the shore and the distant sky-lands,
  Where a ship's dim shape seems etched on
    space,
There lies this cluster of lovely islands,
  Like laughing mermaids grouped in grace.

I look out over the waves and wonder,
  Are they not sirens who dwell in the sea?
When the tide runs high they dip down under
  Like mirthful bathers who sport in glee.

When the tide runs low they lift their shoulders
  Above the billows and gayly spread
Their soft green garments along the boulders
  Of grim gray granite that form their bed.

Close by the group, in sheltered places,
  Many a ship at anchor lies,

And drinks the charm of their smiling faces,
   As lovers drink smiles from maidens' eyes.

But true to the harsh and stern old ocean,
   As maids in a harem are true to one,
They give him all of their hearts' devotion,
   Though wooed forever by moon and sun.

A ship sails on that has bravely waded
   Through foaming billows to sue in vain;
A whip-poor-will flies that has serenaded
   And sung unanswered his plaintive strain.

In the sea's great arms I see them lying,
   Bright and beaming and fond and fair,
While the jealous July day is dying
   In a crimson fury of mad despair.

The desolate moon drifts slowly over,
   And covers its face with the lace of a cloud,
While the sea, like a glad triumphant lover,
Clasps close his islands and laughs aloud.

MY GRAVE.

IF, when I die, I must be buried, let
  No cemetery engulph me—no lone grot,
Where the great palpitating world comes not,
Save when, with heart bowed down and eyelids wet,
It pays its last sad melancholy debt
To some outjourneying pilgrim.   May my lot
Be rather to lie in some much-used spot,
Where human life, with all its noise and fret,
Throbs on about me.   Let the roll of wheels,
With all earth's sounds of pleasure, commerce, love,
And rush of hurrying feet surge o'er my head.
Even in my grave I shall be one who feels
Close kinship with the pulsing world above;
And too deep silence would distress me, dead.

REFUTED.

"Anticipation is sweeter than realization."

I T may be, yet I have not found it so.
   In those first golden dreams of future fame
   I did not find such happiness as came
When toil was crowned with triumph. Now I know
My words have recognition and will go
   Straight to some listening heart my early aim
   To win the idle glory of a name
Pales like a candle in the noonday's glow.

So with the deeper joys of which I dreamed:
   Life yields more rapture than did childhood's fan-
      cies,
   And each year brings more pleasure than I waited.
Friendship proves truer than of old it seemed,
   And, all beyond youth's passion-hued romances,
   Love is more perfect than anticipated.

THE LOST LAND.

THERE is a story of a beauteous land,
        Where fields were fertile and where flowers
            were bright;
Where tall towers glistened in the morning light,
Where happy children wandered hand in hand,
Where lovers wrote their names upon the sand.

They say it vanished from all human sight,
The hungry sea devoured it in a night.

You doubt the tale? ah, you will understand;
For, as men muse upon that fable old,
They give sad credence always at the last,
However they have caviled at its truth,
When with a tear-dimmed vision they behold,
Swift sinking in the ocean of the Past,
The lovely lost Atlantis of their Youth.

THE SOUTH.

A QUEEN of indolence and idle grace,
　　Robed in the vestments of a costly gown,
She turns the languor of her lovely face
　　Upon progression with a lazy frown.

　　Her throne is built upon a marshy down;
Malarial mosses wreathe her like old lace;
　　With slim crossed feet, unshod and bare and brown,
She sits indifferent to the world's swift race.

Across the seas there stalks an ogre grim:
　　Too languid she for even fear's alarms,
　　While frightened nations rally in defence,
She lifts her smiling Creole eyes to him,
　　And reaching out her shapely unwashed arms,
　　She clasps her rightful lover—Pestilence.

A SAILOR'S WIFE.

(HER MEMORY.)

SUN in my lattice, and sun on the sea
   (Oh, but the sun is fair),
And a sky of blue and a sea of green,
And a ship with a white, white sail between,
   And a light wind blowing free—
And back from the stern, and forth from the land,
The last farewell of a waving hand.

Mist on the window and mist on the sea
   (Oh, but the mist is gray),
And the weird, tall shape of a spectral mast
Gleams out of the fog like a ghost of my past,
   And the old hope stirs in me—
The old, old hope that warred with doubt,
While the years with the tides surged in and out.

Rain on my window and rain on the sea
  (Oh, but the rain is sad),
And only the dreams of a vanished barque
And a vanished youth shine through the dark,
  And torture the night and me.
But somewhere, I think, near some fair strand,
That lost ship lies with its waving hand.

LIFE'S JOURNEY.

AS we speed out of youth's sunny station,
　　The track seems to shine in the light,
But it suddenly shoots over chasms
　　Or sinks into tunnels of night.
And the hearts that were brave in the morning
　　Are filled with repining and fears,
As they pause at the City of Sorrow
　　Or pass through the Valley of Tears.

But the road of this perilous journey
　　The hand of the Master has made;
With all its discomforts and dangers,
　　We need not be sad or afraid.
Paths leading from light into darkness,
　　Ways plunging from gloom to despair,
Wind out through the tunnels of midnight
　　To fields that are blooming and fair.

Though the rocks and the shadows surround us,
  Though we catch not one gleam of the day,
Above us fair cities are laughing,
  And dipping white feet in some bay.
And always, eternal, forever,
  Down over the hills in the west,
The last final end of our journey,
  There lies the Great Station of Rest.

'Tis the Grand Central point of all railways,
  All roads unite here when they end;
'Tis the final resort of all tourists,
  All rival lines meet here and blend.
All tickets, all mile-books, all passes,
  If stolen or begged for or bought,
On whatever road or division,
  Will bring you at last to this spot.

If you pause at the City of Trouble,
  Or wait in the Valley of Tears,

Be patient, the train will move onward,
   And rush down the track of the years.
Whatever the place is you seek for,
   Whatever your game or your quest,
You shall come at the last with rejoicing,
   To the beautiful City of Rest.

You shall store all your baggage of worries,
   You shall feel perfect peace in this realm,
You shall sail with old friends on fair waters,
   With joy and delight at the helm.
You shall wander in cool, fragrant gardens
   With those who have loved you the best,
And the hopes that were lost in life's journey
   You shall find in the City of Rest.

THE DISAPPOINTED.

THERE are songs enough for the hero
　　Who dwells on the heights of fame;
I sing for the disappointed—
　　For those who missed their aim.

I sing with a tearful cadence
　　For one who stands in the dark,
And knows that his last, best arrow
　　Has bounded back from the mark.

I sing for the breathless runner,
　　The eager, anxious soul,
Who falls with his strength exhausted,
　　Almost in sight of the goal;

For the hearts that break in silence,
　　With a sorrow all unknown,
For those who need companions,
　　Yet walk their ways alone.

There are songs enough for the lovers
   Who share love's tender pain,
I sing for the one whose passion
   Is given all in vain.

For those whose spirit comrades
   Have missed them on the way,
I sing, with a heart o'erflowing,
   This minor strain to-day.

And I know the Solar system
   Must somewhere keep in space
A prize for that spent runner
   Who barely lost the race.

For the plan would be imperfect
   Unless it held some sphere
That paid for the toil and talent
   And love that are wasted here.

FISHING.

MAYBE this is fun, sitting in the sun,
　　With a book and parasol, as my Angler wishes,
While he dips his line in the ocean brine,
　Under the impression that his bait will catch the
　　fishes.

'Tis romantic, yes, but I must confess

　Thoughts of shady rooms at home somehow seem
　　more inviting.
But I dare not move—"Quiet, there, my love!"
　Says my Angler, "for I think a monster fish is bit-
　　ing."

Oh, of course it's bliss, but how hot it is!
　And the rock I'm sitting on grows harder every
　　minute;
Still my fisher waits, trying various baits,
　But the basket at his side I see has nothing in it.

10

Oh, it's just the way to pass a July day,

    Arcadian and sentimental, dreamy, idle, charming,

But how fierce the sunlight falls! and the way that
      insect crawls

    Along my neck and down my back is really quite
      alarming.

"Any luck?" I gently ask of the angler at his task,

    "There's something pulling at my line," he says;
      "I've almost caught it."

But when with blistered face, we our homeward steps
      retrace,

    We take the little basket just as empty as we
      brought it.

A PIN.

OH, I know a certain lady who is reckoned with
the good,

Yet she fills me with more terror than a raging lion
would.

The little chills run up and down my spine whene'er
we meet,

Though she seems a gentle creature, and she's very
trim and neat.

And she has a thousand virtues and not one acknowl-
edged sin,

But she is the sort of person you could liken to a pin.

And she pricks you and she sticks you in a way that
can't be said.

If you seek for what has hurt you—why, you cannot
find the head!

But she fills you with discomfort and exasperating
pain.

If anybody asks you why, you really can't explain!

A pin is such a tiny thing, of that there is no doubt,

Yet when it's sticking in your flesh you're wretched
    till it's out.

She is wonderfully observing— when she meets a
    pretty girl,
She is always sure to tell her if her hair is out of curl;
And she is so sympathetic to her friend who's much
    admired,
She is often heard remarking, "Dear, you look so
    worn and tired."

And she is an honest critic, for on yesterday she eyed
The new dress I was airing with a woman's natural
    pride,
And she said, "Oh, how becoming!" and then gently
    added, "it
Is really a misfortune that the basque is such a fit."

Then she said, "If you had heard me yester eve, I'm
    sure, my friend,
You would say I was a champion who knows how to
    defend."

And she left me with the feeling—most unpleasant, I
  aver—
That the whole world would despise me if it hadn't
  been for her.

Whenever I encounter her, in such a nameless way
She gives me the impression I am at my worst that
  day.
And the hat that was imported (and which cost me
  half a sonnet),
With just one glance from her round eyes becomes a
  Bowery bonnet.

She is always bright and smiling, sharp and pointed
  for a thrust.
Use does not seem to blunt her point, nor does she
  gather rust,
Oh! I wish some hapless specimen of mankind would
  begin
To tidy up the world for me, by picking up this pin!

THE ACTOR.

OH, man, with your wonderful dower,
   Oh, woman, with genius and grace,
You can teach the whole world with your power,
   If you are but worthy the place.
The stage is a force and a factor
   In moulding the thought of the day,
If only the heart of the actor
   Is high as the theme of the play.

No discourse or sermon can reach us
   Through feeling to reason like you;
No author can stir us and teach us
   With lessons as subtle and true.
Your words and your gestures obeying
   We weep or rejoice with your part,
And the player, behind all his playing,
   He ought to be great as his art.

No matter what role you are giving,
　No matter what skill you betray,
The everyday life you are living,

　Is certain to color the play.
The thoughts we call secret and hidden
　Are creatures of malice, in fact.
They steal forth unseen and unbidden,
　And permeate motive and act.

The genius that shines like a comet
　Fills only one part of God's plan,
If the lesson the world derives from it
　Is marred by the life of the man.
Be worthy your work if you love it;
　The king should be fit for the crown;
Stand high as your art, or above it,
　And make us look up and not down.

ILLOGICAL.

S HE stood beside me while I gave an order
                    for a bonnet.
She shuddered when I said, "And put a
                    bright bird's wing upon it."

A member of the Audubon Society was she;
And cutting were her comments made on
                    worldly folks like me.

She spoke about the helpless birds we wickedly
                    were harming;
She quoted the statistics, and they really
                    were alarming;

She said God meant His little birds to sing
                    in trees and skies;
And there was pathos in her voice, and
                    tears were in her eyes.

"Oh, surely in this beauteous world you
                    can find lovely things
Enough to trim your hats," she said, "with
                    out the dear birds' wings."

I sat beside her that same day, in her
                    own house at dinner,
Angelic being that she was to entertain
                    a sinner!

Her well-appointed table groaned
                    beneath the ample spread
Course followed appetizing course, and
                    hunger sated fled;

But still my charming hostess urged, "Do
                    have a reed-bird, dear,
They are so delicate and sweet
                    at this time of the year."

NEW YEAR.

I SAW on the hills of the morning,
   The form of the New Year arise,
He stood like a statue adorning
   The world with a background of skies.
There were courage and grace in his beautiful face,
   And hope in his glorious eyes.

"I come from Time's boundless forever,"
   He said, with a voice like a song.
"I come as a friend to endeavor,
   I come as a foe to all wrong.
To the sad and afraid I bring promise of aid,
   And the weak I will gird and make strong.

"I bring you more blessings than terrors,
   I bring you more sunlight than gloom,

I tear out your page of old errors,
  And hide them away in Time's tomb.
I reach you clean hands, and lead on to the lands
  Where the lilies of peace are in bloom."

NEW YEAR.

AS the old year sinks down in Time's ocean,
　　Stand ready to launch with the new,
And waste no regrets, no emotion,
　　As the masts and the spars pass from view.
Weep not if some treasures go under,
　　And sink in the rotten ship's hold,
That blithe bonny barque sailing yonder
　　May bring you more wealth than the old.

For the world is forever improving,
　　All the past is not worth one to-day,
And whatever deserves our true loving.
　　Is stronger than death or decay.
Old love, was it wasted devotion?
　　Old friends, were they weak or untrue?
Well, let them sink there in mid ocean,
　　And gaily sail on to the new.

Throw overboard toil misdirected,
   Throw overboard ill-advised hope,
With aims which, your soul has detected,
   Have self as their centre and scope.
Throw overboard useless regretting
   For deeds which you cannot undo,
And learn the great art of forgetting
   Old things which embitter the new.

Sing who will of dead years departed,
   I shroud them and bid them adieu,
And the song that I sing, happy-hearted,
   Is a song of the glorious new.

NOW.

ONE looks behind him to some vanished time
  And says, "Ah, I was happy then, alack!
I did not know it was my life's best prime—
  Oh, if I could go back!"

Another looks, with eager eyes aglow,
  To some glad day of joy that yet will dawn,
And sighs, "I shall be happy then, I know;
  Oh, let me hurry on."

But I—I look out on my fair To-day;
  I clasp it close and kiss its radiant brow,
Here with the perfect present let me stay,
  For I am happy now!